SPORT SUCCESS
Winning Women in Basketball

Marlene Targ Brill

Photo Credits:
Chapter One: FPG International
Chapters Three–Six and cover: Duomo Photography, Inc.

Chapter Two line art by Bob Dorsey

All inquiries should be addressed to:
Barron's Educational Series, Inc.
250 Wireless Boulevard
Hauppauge, NY 11788
http://www.barronseduc.com

Library of Congress Catalog Card No.: 99-88679
International Standard Book No.: 0-7641-1232-5

Library of Congress Cataloging-in-Publication Data

Brill, Marlene Targ.
Winning women in basketball / Marlene Targ Brill.
p. cm. —(Sport success)
Includes bibliographical references (p.) and index.
Summary: An overview of the history of women's basketball, how the game is played, and the equipment, as well as biographies of four notable female players.
ISBN 0-7641-1232-5
1. Basketball players—United States—Biography—Juvenile literature. 2. Women basketball players—United States—Biography—Juvenile literature. 3. Basketball for women—Juvenile literature. [1. Basketball players. 2. Women—Biography. 3. Basketball for women.] I. Title.

GV884.A1 B75 2000 99-88679

PRINTED IN THE UNITED STATES OF AMERICA
9 8 7 6 5 4 3 2 1

Contents

Acknowledgments

Many people helped me gather information for this book. I wish to thank Charles McBride, Youth Basketball of America; Nanci Young, Smith College; Karen Mason, Iowa University Library; Laronica Conway, NCAA; Frank Scott, Morningside High School; Wendy Border, agent; Dennis Sampier, Detroit Shock; Jim Jarrett and Debbie Byrne, Old Dominion University; Billie Moore, Hall of Famer and former Olympic coach; Lyndon Hardin, South Plains Junior College; Megan Boniface, Houston Comets; Pat Summit, former Olympian, Hall of Famer, and University of Tennessee coach; Jody Hoatson, University of Connecticut communications; Jim Vincent, Southwick-Tolland High School.

A special thank-you goes to Nancy Lieberman-Cline, Hall of Famer, Women's Sports Foundation president, and Detroit Shock coach, and Sheryl Swoopes, Houston Comets.

A Note to Readers

Once upon a time there were girls who loved to run, shoot baskets, speed skate, race bicycles and cars, and climb to great heights. These girls were different from active females today. Instead of being applauded for their talents, they were told they *couldn't* and *shouldn't* play most sports.

As recently as the late 1800s, adults offered a host of reasons why girls should stick to their dolls and needlework. One reason followed the belief that exercise hurt the frail female body and tired the mind. For example, some doctors assumed that riding caused "bicycle face," a scrunched-up look that supposedly came from the strain of sitting forward on a bicycle seat. Most likely, the tight corsets, high collars, and big hats of the day led to the frowns.

Another common myth suggested that females who played like boys had something wrong with them. For one thing, active girls *looked* unladylike. Baron Pierre de Coubertin, founder of the modern Olympics, wrote in 1896: "It is indecent that spectators should be exposed to the risk of a woman being smashed before their very eyes."

Other critics assumed that females could never be as good in sports as males anyway. Therefore, they wondered, why would girls even bother to try? Such faultfinders called girls who played sports *tomboys* just because they wanted to have the same fun as boys.

Similar negative views of women in sports lingered into the 1960s. By then, females had started pushing for equal rights at home and at work. This led to Americans accepting that women and girls performed well in specific sports, such as gymnastics and figure skating.

Then the United States Congress passed the important Title IX law in 1972. Title IX ordered schools to give girls the same opportunities as boys to participate in sports. This meant that teams, equipment, and *all* sports had to be open to girls. Not long after the United States ruling, Canada and Australia passed similar laws. Each country required their schools to budget equal money for boys' and girls' sports. These laws championed the wild notion that girls would succeed if given the chance.

Little by little, schools began programming certain sports for girls. Some girls joined all-boy teams. Others battled to organize teams and leagues of their own. Gradually, females broke down barriers in sports such as sailboat racing, mountain climbing, wheelchair racing, coaching, and snowboarding that were mostly male-only arenas. Athletic girls who were once told to watch or cheerlead could now win their own medals.

At the same time girls entered more sports, new research replaced old-fashioned thinking that had kept girls on the sidelines. The Institute for Athletics and Education and the President's

Council on Physical Fitness discovered that active girls earned better grades and were three times more likely to graduate from high school than their less active sisters. Girls who played sports were also more likely to go on to college and remain healthier as adults, developing fewer health problems, such as heart disease. In 1999, the Big Ten College Conference reported that a record 80 percent of women leaders in the top 500 U.S. companies participated in sports. These figures showed that girls who played sports felt better about themselves. They developed more confidence all-around because sports taught them what it means to be strong in body and mind.

Updated studies plus Title IX have had an amazing impact on girls participating in sports. In 1972, only 1 of every 27 girls joined high school sports. Today, 1 in 3 girls participate, reflecting an upward trend in women's athletics. Now more girls play soccer than the number of girls who joined all sports in 1970. Consider, too, that in 1972 only 96 women athletes from the United States competed in the summer Olympics. By the summer of 1996, the roster had climbed to 280 women.

The 1996 and 1998 U.S. Women Olympic winners for soccer, baseball, basketball, and ice hockey—all new Olympic sports—were loaded with players who got their start on high school and college teams because of Title IX. These players confirm the success of 20 years of giving girls the opportunity to strut their sport's stuff. Now that's progress!

Still, we have a long way to go toward equality for women in sports. One group to win over is the media. Except for sports such as golf, ice skating, tennis, gymnastics, and now basketball, women athletes are invisible in most newspapers, television stations, and books. Donna Lopiano, former director of the Women's Sports Foundation, reported: "Until the 1990s, sports pages devoted more column inches to horses and dogs than to women's sports."

A 1996 study from Vanderbilt University confirmed Ms. Lopiano's findings. Researchers found that women received only 7 to 11 percent of national newspaper sports coverage. Television networks focused on skating, gymnastics, Olympic highlights, or special events. Otherwise, women in sports were mostly invisible to the media.

Little has changed with media coverage going into the twenty-first century. The joys and talents of women athletes in many sports have gone unsung for too long. This book series seeks to broadcast the news that active girls and women are involved in all sports. So, find the sport in the series that interests you most. Learn how other athletes have succeeded, often bucking great odds. Read how these talented athletes have fought battles so you can play any sport you choose. Then go out and play! Join the winning women and girls everywhere who are just warming up for a future of SPORT SUCCESS.

Marlene Targ Brill

Chapter One

On Your Mark, Get Set . . .

Basketball is one of the few truly American team games. It was invented by an American in America for Americans. The game was originally created for men. Yet sport lovers have found a way for women to play almost since the first basket was sunk.

A Bold, New Invention

In 1891, Canadian-born James Naismith needed a way to perk up his physical education class. He taught at the International Young Men's Christian Association (YMCA) Training School, now Springfield College, which trained instructors for YMCAs nationwide. The men hated the indoor marches and drills during the cold winter months. So Naismith tried to adapt several outdoor games, such as football and baseball, for inside play. Each game proved too rough for the limited gym space.

Then Naismith had one more idea, this time for a brand new game. To control the game, Naismith chose a large ball to be thrown rather than smacked with a bat or stick. He also wanted to curb a player's running with the ball. He figured that without running there would be no reason to chase or tackle another player, as in football. This would keep players from getting too rowdy.

Naismith still needed a reason to play. After some thinking, he decided that a goal box should sit at each end of the floor to catch the balls. One team could sink the ball into their opponent's goal. Now Naismith worried that a pushy defense would crowd around the goal. So he lifted the goals above everyone's head.

Naismith never found the two boxes he wanted for goals. Instead, the school janitor gave him two old peach baskets from the storeroom. Naismith hammered the baskets to the lower railing of the gym balcony 10 feet above the floor, the height of hoops today.

Afterward, Naismith posted 13 rules on a bulletin board inside the gym entrance. Many of these rules still govern the game of basketball. The original game called for any number of players. Because Naismith's first class happened to have 18 students, the first basketball game had 9 players on a team. On a wintry January day in 1892, bumbling athletes tried to run, dribble, shoot, and block each other to get a mushy soccer ball into the raised basket. One student suggested calling the new game Naismith ball. Naismith preferred a simpler name: basket ball.

New Game Gains Fans

Basketball turned into an instant success. Students liked the lively game, often telling classmates about the fun they were having in gym. The school newspaper, the *Triangle*, printed the rules. Within a month, Naismith had organized a game between two different YMCA teams. News of this exciting game spread around town, eventually reaching faraway YMCAs.

Teachers from Buckingham Grade School saw a basketball practice and formed a girls' team. Then a

Smith College gym teacher, Senda Berenson, read an article Naismith had written. She considered introducing basketball to her students. Berenson agreed with the new thinking of the day that encouraged team play for girls. She believed that competitive games developed "quickness of judgment and action, and physical and moral self-control." But she clung to some of the same fears as those who opposed women playing any sports, especially a "man's sport."

"The desire to win and the excitement of the game will make our women do sadly unwomanly things," she wrote.

Girls' Rules

To prevent the harmful effects of competition, Berenson devised special rules. These rules limited the amount of running and competition. More important, they discouraged roughness that looked so unladylike and caused "dangerous nervous tendencies."

"Two important changes are the division of the playing field and prohibiting of snatching or batting the ball from the hands of another player," Berenson wrote in *Basket Ball for Women.*

According to her rules, two players per team played on one third of the court. Girls could only hold the ball for three seconds and were allowed just three dribbles in a row. Stealing or knocking the ball from someone's hands was out of the question. Moreover, these games were only for girls. Before each game,

Berenson posted this sign: "Notice! Gentlemen are not allowed in the gymnasium during basketball games. S. Berenson."

Berenson's tighter rules appealed to parents, school officials, and women at other colleges. In 1895, Clara Gregory Baer brought girls' basketball to the proper Sophie Newcomb College in New Orleans. Teachers called a two-handed throw a *foul* because they believed it forced shoulders forward, causing "a consequent flattening of the chest." To avoid flat chests, women at Newcomb developed a one-hand setup shot.

Newcomb women played the first public game in front of 560 delighted females, in keeping with the usual ban on male viewers. The game proved so popular that Baer printed *Basquette*, the first published set of rules for women. In 1901, Baer became editor of the first women's basketball publication, *Basket Ball for Women*, by the Spalding Athletic Library.

Women Take to Basketball

On April 14, 1896, the Stanford University women's basketball team beat University of California (at Berkeley) women 2–1. This game was the first women's basketball competition between two colleges. Similar to Smith and Newcomb, Berkeley women refused to play before men. But 500 female fans cheered the close contest, and the *San Francisco Examiner* covered the event. "The fighting was hard and the playing was good. The girls jumped, scrambled, and fell over one another on the floor, but they didn't mind. They were up quick as a flash, chasing after the ball again."

Reports of these early games encouraged schoolgirls everywhere to take to courts. Like their basketball brothers, they were sometimes called "cagers." The name came from the wire cages that often surrounded basketball courts to prevent wild dives for balls thrown into balconies. Another safeguard from the balcony crowd was the addition of backboards behind the baskets. These kept eager fans from dangling their feet and kicking balls out of the basket.

Unlike male athletes, however, women played in tight-fitting clothes of the day. Whereas men ran from end to end on the court in short pants and sleeveless shirts, women squeezed into boney corsets for underwear and covered themselves from neck to feet. Girls played in high, dark stockings; full divided skirts called bloomers; high-neck, long-sleeve blouses; and soft, slipper-like shoes. At game's end, hair pins and dainty linen handkerchiefs littered the gym floor. Not the best outfits to wear when changing positions quickly, running, and shooting baskets!

Trouble for Women's Basketball

Men earned money from basketball in 1895. From then on, professional leagues came and went. Players switched leagues and teams as one folded and

Underhand shots were popular among overdressed bloomer girls in 1899.

another prospered. Meanwhile, basketball madness spread—around the country and overseas. In 1904, men's basketball became an Olympic sport. In years to come, the men's game would attract fans in almost every country. Then the Basketball Association of America melted into the National Basketball Association (NBA) in 1949. Professional athletes found a lasting organization that would mold men's basketball into the big business it is today.

Women had their share of basketball successes, too. But girls and women continued to fight many uphill battles just for the right to play. Once basketball caught on in women's colleges, cries grew louder against "well-bred young ladies running and falling, shrieking in excitement, and calling each other by nicknames." Watered-down rules, cut programs, and bad press dogged women's basketball.

A March 1912 *Ladies Home Journal* article questioned: "Are Athletics Making Girls Masculine?" In the 1918 *Official Basket Ball Guide for Women*, Dr. J. Anna Norris advised girls not to play basketball during the first three days of their period. One *Los Angeles Times* article titled "Sweet Things Have Scrap" reported how a high school game resulted in hair pulling and other rowdiness. "There was something disquieting in the grim and murderous determinations with which the young ladies chased each other all over the court."

From the first girls' game, physical education teachers struggled to counteract basketball's image as unwomanly. One way was to link games with other social events. Senda Berenson served snacks or fancy dinners after Smith games. These activities became known as the "Cookies and Milk" strategy. As late as the 1930s, teams connected basketball with beauty contests.

Even with these setbacks, women's basketball spread worldwide. In 1921, teams from Italy, England, France, Norway, and Switzerland competed in the Jeux Olympiques Femines in Monaco. Women's basketball wouldn't enter the Olympics until 1976.

But more girls everywhere were seeing how much fun playing basketball could be. By 1925, 37 states were running high school tournaments. Each used the newer open-bottom baskets. Before then, basketball officials hand released the ball with pull chains attached to a trap door on the bottom of the basket.

Women's Basketball Gets Organized

The Amateur Athletic Union (AAU) had set standards for men's nonschool sports teams since 1888. In 1926, the AAU sponsored the first national women's basketball championship. This groundbreaking contest came as schools throughout the country debated the value of women competing in any sport. One by one, colleges eliminated competitions as a waste of time and wiped out women's programs. In 1927, the national organization for physical education teachers and state health directors decreed: "We go on record as being opposed to national and statewide tournaments for girls."

The AAU involvement gave girls' basketball the boost it needed. This was the only group keeping the game alive on a large scale throughout the 1930s. As amateur and company-sponsored teams slowly filled the gap left by high schools and colleges, the AAU organized the games and championships that allowed these teams to flourish.

The All American Red Heads proved one of the more colorful amateur teams. Everyone on the team was required to have red hair "by God or by bottle."

Beginning in 1936 until the 1980s, some form of the Red Heads traveled the country playing men's teams under men's rules. Over the years, thousands of people flocked to see their skillful ball handling. At one game, 17,500 fans filled the Chicago Stadium. "These women are as deft at handling the ball as they are at lipstick," commented a television announcer who thought this was a compliment.

Company Teams

During World War II, record numbers of women replaced soldiers in offices and factories. The number of company women's basketball teams soared. Competition for the best players was great, but players had to look as good as they played. Companies attracted crowds by outfitting their players in skimpy

Hazel Walker

One of the most talented players of the 1930s and 1940s was Hazel Walker, a young Cherokee woman. Hazel captured 11 AAU All-American titles with different teams. Her Hazel Walker Arkansas Travelers won the hearts of basketball lovers nationwide. Hazel and her teammates shot hoops nightly for seven months, playing each game in a different town. Townspeople often looked down on women traveling alone by car. But once they discovered that top athletes could act like ladies too, fans flocked to Hazel's games.

uniforms and requiring them to wear makeup and curl their hair. Sexy photos emphasized the fact that companies viewed their players more as pinup girls than athletes.

The *Philadelphia Tribune* sponsored one of the better-known company teams. The all-black Tribune Girls challenged men's teams in gyms and schoolyards throughout the United States. The best part was they usually won. The Tribune Girls lost only six games in nine years.

Hanes Hosiery sponsored another winning team. From 1947 until 1951, the Hanes women played an amazing four years of 102 straight wins. Their run lasted until the Hutchinson Flying Queens from Wayland Baptist College bested them with 131 straight wins during the 1950s.

The most successful AAU team in history was from the Nashville Business College (NBC). Nashville won 11 AAU championships from 1950 to 1969. The team's leading player, Nera White, was selected most valuable player at AAU national tournaments 10 times and made AAU All-American 15 times. She was the first woman inducted into the Naismith Basketball Hall of Fame in Springfield, Massachusetts, which later separated into the Women's Basketball Hall of Fame in Knoxville, Tennessee.

White and Nashville probably would have continued to thrive had the AAU not changed the rules. To speed up the game, the AAU allowed five players, unlimited dribbling, and stealing. NBC president, Herman O. Balls, opposed the new rules and dropped the team in 1969. "It is well known that my team will never play men's rules," he raged. "I think it is wrong and if persisted in, will eventually destroy girls' basketball."

Bring on Title IX

Nera White and other athletes from company teams provided the backbone of the new U.S. national team. In 1953, the U.S. team beat Chile 49–36 in the first women's world championship held in Santiago, Chile. Four years later, the U.S. team topped the Soviet Union 51–48 in front of 40,000 cheering fans in Rio de Janeiro, Brazil. Most of the nation had no idea that women played or won. Television was still too new to be in many homes, and sports reporters had more important stories to follow—about men.

The 1970s brought major changes in women's basketball. In 1971, the 30-second shot clock was introduced. The same year the wise men of basketball finally realized that girls had enough energy to run the entire court and dribble as needed. The biggest change, however, came after Congress passed Title IX in 1972. Girls suddenly had opportunities that were never available to them before to play basketball in school. Hopes ran high for more teams, better equipment, and scholarships. Women's coaches dreamed of no longer working two jobs to pay the bills.

Making a law was one thing. Changing long-ingrained attitudes was another. Men's basketball and football dominated most school and professional programs. Men feared they would be forced to give up limited funding to make room for girls' basketball. The difficult task of proving that women's basketball could be profitable and draw crowds began.

Growth of Women's Basketball

Women's basketball did better on the international scene. In 1976, the Fédération Internationale de Basketball Amateur (FIBA), the agency that governs international basketball competition, added the first Olympic six-team women's basketball event. The news brought smiles to countless U.S. women who labored unnoticed on local teams with nowhere to go with their talents.

When tryouts for the first Olympic games in Montreal were announced, clinics were held around the country for women to try out. More than 250 girls crammed into the Queens College gym in New York City alone. After a series of tryouts, the U.S. national team was announced. Two players stood out. Ann Meyers of California, the first high school player on any national team, and eighteen-year-old Nancy Lieberman made the Olympic team. When the United States took home its first silver medal, Nancy became the youngest basketball player to earn an Olympic honor. Ann went on to become the first woman to sign with the all-male NBA.

After the Olympics, promoters tried to capitalize on the new popularity of women's basketball. In 1978, the Women's Professional Basketball League was established with eight teams. Three seasons later, the league fizzled. As with the early men's game, women's professional leagues came and went. The Women's American Basketball Association (1984–85) and Liberty Basketball Association (1992) each folded before their first season ended. The only way skilled American women could earn a living playing basketball was to leave home for an overseas team. Italy, France, and Norway offered U.S. players more money and fame than they could ever imagine at home. Women's basketball seemed valued in these countries.

The 1996 Olympics in Atlanta, Georgia

The 1996 Olympics provided the spark women's basketball needed to blossom at home. Women's softball and soccer were two new Olympic sports, which helped focus attention on all women's team sports for the first time. Unlike earlier competitions, this one provided the 1996 women's basketball team with backing, money, and tryouts almost a year before the games. Now teammates had time to get to know each other and practice together. Moreover, they got paid enough to concentrate on basketball. Women left full-time jobs and teams overseas for the chance to play at home for the United States.

To prepare for the Olympics, the national team faced a killer schedule. The idea was to parade their sport across the nation to build a fan base. With so many individual stars, another goal was to build team unity. The women practiced for three months to prepare for the 52-game schedule against college, ama-

The 6'2" Chamique Holdsclaw led the University of Tennessee to three straight national championships (1996–1998), earned four-time college All-American, and took her game to another level with the U.S. national team and WNBA Washington Mystics.

teur, and overseas teams. For nine months, they traveled nationwide and to China, Russia, and Australia. At each stop, they drilled, held interviews and clinics, weight lifted and conditioned, and played a game. Then they started the routine over again in another city.

"Women have had to be a little nicer, work a little harder ... than men to nurture fan-player relationships," sports writer Christine Brennan noted in *Women's Sports & Fitness*. "As in business, when you work hard for the customer, they notice. And they come back."

The strategy worked. The team went into the Olympics with a 52–0 winning streak. Along the way, they attracted record numbers of fans nationwide who respected their skills. Reporters started calling the women the "Dream Team" after the men's Olympic gold medal team.

Full of confidence, the U.S. womenís basketball team exploded onto the Olympic scene. They played eight games before increasingly larger crowds. Cheering fans waved American flags and signs that said "The REAL Dream Team." By the final game, almost 35,000 fans celebrated the 111–87 win over Brazil. The Olympic gold was a dream come true.

"This is a great day for women's basketball," U.S. forward Sheryl Swoopes told reporters.

League Ups and Downs

The Olympic gold medal and growing interest in college basketball fueled the flames of another professional women's league. Within a year, the eight-team American Basketball League (ABL) burst onto the sport scene full of hope for women's basketball. For the first time, talented women basketball players had a place to earn a living in the United States. Now there was a league that treated its players as professionals, giving them $50,000 to $150,000 in salary. The number wasn't what men earned, but it was getting closer.

Then the NBA announced its Women's National Basketball Association (WNBA). From the beginning, the ABL couldn't compete. With NBA pull, the WNBA received the few corporate sponsors and television contracts interested in women's sports. Even though ABL games averaged 4,500 fans each, the league folded on December 22, 1998. Ninety players, ten coaches, and thousands of fans lost their favorite teams.

Meanwhile, the eight-team WNBA achieved amazing success. By the 2000 season, the league had grown to 16 teams, with the promise of more to come. The added teams opened doors to ABL players who had lost their jobs.

"The league has been strengthened since the ABL folded," said Coach Linda Hill-MacDonald of the Cleveland Rockers. "The experience ABL players brought to the WNBA has been a real benefit."

The WNBA proved so hot that the teams attracted international players from faraway countries like Russia, Mozambique, and Australia. In previous years, Americans had found that the only place to play was overseas. The situation seemed to be reversing. By the end of its second season, the WNBA included 31 players from 21 different countries.

The Future of Women's Basketball

The future holds great promise for women's basketball. According to the National Sporting Goods Association, basketball leads the way in the growing world of girls' sports. Cable television stations now broadcast women's college and professional basketball games regularly, which promotes greater acceptance of women's basketball among the public.

More than 14.1 million girls play basketball in the United States alone. In 1999, girls from ages 7 to 17 played 17 percent more basketball than they did in 1990, and the numbers keep climbing. More than 205 colleges nationwide support women's basketball teams for those who want to continue playing after high school.

These figures mean a lot to basketball-loving girls growing up in a new century. Young girls can imagine competing on organized teams as their skills improve. High school athletes can hope for scholarships like their basketball-playing brothers. College girls, too, can dream of professional and national teams. Why? Because they see women who braved some tough times just to play the sport they loved. They see winning women achieve sport success in basketball.

Chapter Two

How to Play

Basketball is an exciting game. It is fast paced and action packed. Players are always on the move. When creating girls' basketball, Senda Berenson wrote: "The game is too quick, too vigorous, the action too continuous. ... In one moment a person must judge space and time in order to run and catch the ball at the right place, must decide to whom it may best be thrown, and at the same time just remember not to 'foul'."

The Players

With basketball, two teams play together on a court. A coach organizes and guides each team. One to three referees enforce the rules of the game for the players. Five players from each team try to score points by sinking a ball into their opponent's basket. At the same time, they scramble to prevent the other team from getting the ball in their basket and scoring. The team with the most points—and baskets—at the end of the game wins.

The Court. Although basketball is a team sport, anyone can enjoy practicing alone. All someone needs is a ball, smooth court, basket, and a little imagination. Then shooting hoops on a concrete driveway turns into a game in a crowded basketball stadium.

The size of basketball courts and height of the baskets vary according to who plays. Most school courts measure 84 feet (25 meters) long by 50 feet (15 meters) wide. Colorful wooden WNBA courts stretch

94 feet (28.7 meters) long by 50 feet (15 meters) wide. Baskets are raised with the age of the players. At WNBA games, the basket hangs 10 feet (3 meters) off the floor at each end.

The metal rim on the baskets is 18 inches (45.7 centimeters) across. Attached to the rim is a bottomless net that hangs down. The rim is fixed to a wood or thick, hard plastic backboard that measures 6 feet (1.8 meters) wide by 3.5 feet (1 meter) high. In professional games, the backboard is padded at the bottom to keep tall players from getting hurt.

Court Markings. The court is divided lengthwise by a center, or *half-court*, line. The half of the court near the basketball where a team attacks is called the *frontcourt*. The *backcourt* is the half where a team defends its basket.

A *jump circle* line surrounds the middle of the half-court line. One player from each team stands in the circle at the beginning of play and jumps for the first ball.

Lines at the ends and sides of the court mark the overall playing area. Fifteen feet (4.5 meters) into the court from either end line are *free throw*, or *foul lines*. A player shoots unchallenged behind this line after referees call a *foul* against the other team. Meanwhile, teammates and opponents watch from behind lines along the *free-throw lane*. This lined space stretches from the free-throw line to the end line. The lane is also called the *three-second area* because offensive players can only stay here for up to three seconds while the ball is in play.

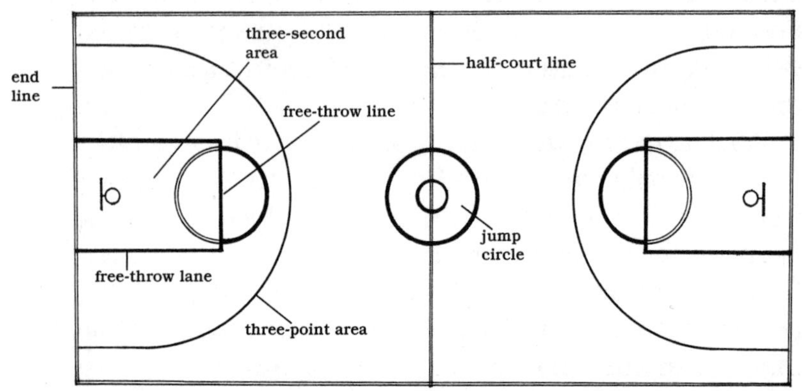

Markings on the basketball court.

An arc around the basket and free-throw lane is called the *three-point line*. Any ball sunk from outside this line earns an extra point—three instead of two—because the shooter is farther from the net.

Positions. All players can grab and move with the ball during a basketball game. To keep teammates from bumping into one another, coaches assign different positions. Each position has a special job that depends upon where the player is on the court. Positions also depend upon a player's height and strength. Even then, jobs change as the team moves from offense, or scoring, to defense, or keeping the other team from scoring. Coaches can replace any player with a substitute from the sidelines.

The three main team positions are *guard*, *forward*, and *center*. Guards are usually the smallest and fastest players. They take the ball up the court, covering the largest area between the half-court and free-throw lines.

Guards must handle the ball well, be alert to passing, and be skilled at long-range shots. Coaches assign either one or two guards per game. When there are two, one is a *point guard*, who handles the ball. The other is a *shooting guard*, who mainly shoots and passes.

Forwards cover the side of the court between the free-throw lines and sidelines. Their job is to score from the sideline and try to snare *rebounds*, missed balls that bounce off the rim or backboard.

Centers play nearest the basket. Usually, they stand with their back to the basket so they can face the court action. Centers are tall or high jumpers who can grab rebounds and sink baskets from close range.

Equipment

Besides a court with a basket and backboard, there is little equipment required for basketball. All a player needs is a ball and comfortable clothes. Teammates usually wear shorts, the same color sleeveless shirts with a number to indicate the player, and athletic shoes. Since basketball involves so much footwork, players find that shoes with good ankle and foot support and thick soles buffer the shock of jumping and running better.

Basketballs are round balls encased with leather, rubber, or manufactured material. They usually measure about 29.5 to 30.75 inches (75 to 78 centimeters) around and weigh between 20 and 22 ounces (567 and 624 grams). Leagues for younger boys and girls use smaller balls.

Moving the Ball

In basketball, the ball is always moved by hand. Players can bounce, throw, tap, or roll the ball in any direction to get it closer to the opponent's basket. They cannot kick the ball, knee it, or slap it with the fist.

Dribbling. This is one skill that separates basketball from other ball games. Dribbling occurs when a player moves while pushing or tapping the ball to the floor, like bouncing. Players dribble to advance the ball up the court. Dribbling allows the ball handler to get in a better position to shoot or pass the ball to a teammate. Before a player takes a step, however, the ball must be released. Then, just one hand at a time performs the dribble.

Players can take any number of steps as long as they keep dribbling the ball. Once they stop, they must pass or shoot the ball. Walking or running while holding the ball is called *traveling*, which is not allowed. If someone dribbles, catches the ball, and dribbles a second time, that player breaks a different rule with a *double dribble*.

Pivoting is the only movement that can occur after a player stops dribbling. Pivoting is stepping with one foot while keeping the other on the ground. Pivoting allows the ball handler to change directions and swing away from oncoming opponents.

Shooting. A team earns points each time a player makes a basket, or *field goal.* Shots taken from outside the three-point line are worth three points. Baskets thrown from inside the three-point line are worth two points.

Players who shoot from free-throw lines receive one point for each basket. A player goes to the free-throw line for a *foul shot* after the official calls a foul by an opposing player. The right to an extra shot comes if a player is fouled while shooting, or if the other team exceeds its number of allotted fouls. In college or international games, players are allowed up to five fouls. The WNBA and NBA allow six before a player must leave the game. Fouls are called on opposing players for pushes, holding, or hitting.

The only way to score points is to sink the ball in the basket. Therefore, developing shooting skills is key to helping a team win games. Good shooting skills

come from being in balance, looking at the basket, and maintaining control of the ball. Three kinds of shots are *layups*, *jump shots*, and *set shots*.

Layups are one way to prepare to shoot the ball after catching a pass or dribbling near the basket. The player who is ready to shoot holds the ball with both hands, brings one foot forward, springs off the other while stretching both arms upward, and then follows the shot with one arm while letting go of the ball. With a jump shot, the shooter leaps straight up off both feet and lets go of the ball at the top of the jump. Jump shots are more difficult for opponents to block because they are released much higher. Most players throw set shots from the free-throw line. Set shots require no jumping. They are taken with both feet firmly on the ground behind the line.

Passing. Good basketball requires that a team control the ball. Passing is the quickest way to move the ball toward the basket and keep it from charging opponents. The type of pass a player chooses depends upon what is happening on the court.

A closely guarded player uses an *overhead pass*. The player holds the ball above the head and throws it hard toward a teammate. A two-handed *chest pass* works when the player has a clear path to the receiver. With a chest pass, the player firmly grasps the ball at chest level and hurls it to a teammate. When there is no clear path between a player and receiver, the player can bounce the ball toward the receiver. The player may pivot to move away from an opponent before making the *bounce pass*.

Game Time

College and professional women's games are divided into two halves. Each half runs for 20 minutes with a 15-minute rest, or halftime, in the middle. Should the game end in a tie, the two teams play five minutes extra, or overtime. If there is still a tie after five minutes, the game continues for five-minute stretches until one team breaks the tie and wins. Some tie games continue with sudden death instead. Here, the winner is the first team to sink a basket.

Timing is different for men's and youth games. Men play four 12-minute periods. High schoolers run and shoot for four 8-minute quarters with 1-minute breaks between the first and third quarters and 10 minutes to rest between halves. Younger teams play 6-minute quarters.

Whichever pass players use, they can fake out opponents by learning to position themselves so opponents cannot tell what they will do next. In the opponent's half of the court, the *triple-threat* works best. A player faces the opponent's basket holding the ball chest high. Opponents never know whether the player will shoot, pass, or dribble.

Basketball seems to have a lot of rules and moves to learn. Once the basics are understood, however, the game flows with remarkable speed. There is constant movement—to get and keep the ball, to shoot the ball. Players race from one end of the court to the other without a break. The action is what draws girls to basketball and keeps them playing as women, just as they have for more than one hundred years.

Here are some of their stories.

Chapter Three

Nancy Lieberman-Cline

Nancy Lieberman-Cline is one of the greats of women's basketball. Almost single-handedly, she forced people to pay attention to the women's game. When she was eighteen, she became the youngest basketball player—male or female—to win an Olympic medal. During college, she turned an underdog team into a winning machine that broke attendance records and put women's college sports on television. After college, her fierce love of the game drove her to the top of every women's professional league. When opportunities for women's basketball faded, Nancy created them. She joined a men's professional league, the first woman to do so. She wrote books and articles, broadcast games, coached—all to put women's basketball on the world map.

Early World of Hoops

Nancy was born on July 1, 1958, in Brooklyn, New York. When she was still a baby, the Lieberman family moved to nearby Far Rockaway. Her father, Jerome, had left her mother, Renee, by the time Nancy was ten. Renee raised her son and daughter alone, staying home with help from Nancy's grandparents.

Unlike her older brother, Nancy was a mover. "Cliff liked to read and listen to music. I always wanted to get out and play," Nancy recalled. "As long as I could remember, I played sports in the schoolyard. By age seven, I was a good athlete, so the boys would choose the girl. That made me feel good."

Nancy's first love was football. She joined a neighborhood team, the Peewees. At the time, her parents were battling through their divorce. "Sports became my way to relieve stress."

But Nancy's mother disapproved of girls playing any sport with boys. Football was way more than she could accept. Renee quickly ended Nancy's budding football career.

Nancy boldly turned her energy toward basketball. When she was ten, she easily made the boys' police athletic league. She was one of the best players to try out. Before the first game, however, officials refused to let her play. They claimed that the team was only insured for boys. In school at P.S. 124, Nancy heard the same thing. No girls allowed.

Nancy never let anyone tell her she couldn't do something. Although nobody in her family ever played sports, Nancy loved to compete. She liked to feel part of a team. Full of drive, the fiery redhead took to the streets. She played basketball with boys in playgrounds, at the beach, in nearby recreation centers. At first, the guys let her play because they needed her equipment. Once they realized how good she was, they accepted her for herself.

Girls Don't Play Basketball

Nancy couldn't get enough of basketball. She was determined to improve herself by playing with the best athletes. Many days, she boarded the A train from Far Rockaway to Harlem, where the best players shot hoops.

Renee never understood her daughter's interest in basketball. Girls don't play sports, she scolded her. Sports were unladylike. Besides, taking the train to Harlem was dangerous.

Nancy begged her mother to let her take the train. If Renee would change her mind, Nancy promised not to hurt anybody. Renee was not amused. She accused Nancy of having something wrong with her. She pleaded with Nancy to give up the game, saying girls had no future in basketball. One day, Renee got so frustrated, she stuck a screwdriver into Nancy's basketball.

"I'm going to make history."

"The worst thing you could say to me as a kid was you can't do this," Nancy explained. "I'm going to prove them wrong. So I said to my mother, 'I'm going to make history.'"

So What If I'm a Tomboy

At Far Rockaway High School, Nancy played softball, volleyball, and her favorite, basketball. She got grief about basketball in school, too. Nancy dove for balls. She pounded her way down the court, charging through opponents. She dominated the games. Everyone complained she played like a boy.

Nancy never cared what people thought. She just wanted to be a great basketball player. She preferred playing more like her heroes, New York Knickerbockers Willis Reed and Walt Frazier, than like girls who shoot balls underhand from between their legs. Nancy wore a number 10 jersey like Frazier and played center because of Reed. But her courage came from watching boxer Muhammad Ali.

"He believed in himself," she told a reporter, "and he always did what he said he would."

When Nancy was 16, a teammate noticed a newspaper article about tryouts for the 1974 national team. Nancy and some friends traveled to nearby Queens College, one of four tryout sites in the country. There they played their hearts out before the judges. At the end of the day, 10 out of 250 high school and college athletes remained. Nancy was one of the ten invited for the next round of tryouts in Albuquerque, New Mexico.

By then, Nancy's basketball playing was well known in Rockaway. People began to notice the gutsy basketball player who was making herself, and their neighborhood, famous. In a show of support, the community raised money to help pay for Nancy's trip. Her high school coach flew with her to New Mexico for five days of competition. Nancy thrilled at the sight of so many talented basketball players.

"After seeing other women playing sports, I knew nothing was wrong with me," Nancy remembered.

The Young Olympian

Nancy broke her ribs during tryouts and had to come home. Before she left, the national coach urged her to work on her game. She wanted Nancy for the

1980 Olympic team. Nancy told her firmly that she would be on the 1976 team. "You don't know me," she said boldly.

Nancy beat her promise. In 1975, the seventeen-year-old made the national team for the Pan-American games. During her first game, she played only ten minutes. Still, she was so excited she barely sat still on the bench. "It was so thrilling," she beamed. "You are playing for your country, wearing the USA. I'll never forget the level of play and competition."

At school, Nancy's Rockaway Seahorses turned into one of the best New York City school teams. But girl's basketball was not challenging enough for Nancy. She joined a boys' Amateur Athletic Union (AAU) team in Harlem. Here teammates called her "Fire" for her hair color and the way she charged opponents. Nancy also led a Catholic Youth Organization team to their league title. Nancy was on a basketball roll nobody could stop. The fancy passes and footwork she learned in Harlem were becoming legendary.

The next year, Nancy missed her high school prom and graduation to play on the U.S. Olympic team. At age eighteen, she became the youngest basketball player—boy or girl—to earn an Olympic medal in Montreal, Canada.

"For her to make the 1976 Olympic team at her age speaks volumes about what kind of a player she was and what people thought about her potential in basketball," said 1976 Olympic coach and Hall of Famer Billie Moore.

As a newcomer, Nancy hardly played on the U.S. team. But Moore sent Nancy into a qualifying game with Bulgaria to act tough, jump, and distract the shooter. Nancy did much more.

"She didn't go by her," Moore joked. "She went *through* her." Nancy ran so fast and jumped so high she kneed the woman in the chest, causing her to fall back and hit her head on the bleachers. She left the court on the stretcher. Then both teams qualified for the Olympics.

"Every time the other girl played, the coach put me in," Nancy said. "She was so afraid of me, she passed the ball. I tell people I had a hand in winning the silver."

College Days

After the Olympics, colleges flooded Nancy with basketball scholarships. The response was incredible for women's basketball. With over one hundred offers, Nancy had her pick of top schools. In the end, she chose Old Dominion (OD), a small school in Norfolk, Virginia a few hours from home. She liked the fact that the Lady Monarchs were an underdog team. She wanted to help build their program.

Again, the faultfinders appeared. "People said you can't go to OD. You'll never win a championship. You'll never be All-American," Nancy bristled. Now she had something to prove.

The 5-foot, 10-inch, 155-pound forward burst onto the court, scoring 30 points a game. With her

Olympic silver medal taped to her leg for good luck, Nancy tried to win games by herself. Then the coach took her aside.

"She said if you would make everybody around you better, we can win championships," Nancy recalled. "If we win, you will be rewarded."

Nancy followed the coach's advice, and a crazy thing happened. The first two years she averaged 20 points a game, and the Lady Monarchs just missed the national championships. The third year, Nancy's shooting average dropped to 12 points a game. Yet, the team won 37 games, lost only one, and won its first national. In the fourth year, Nancy averaged 10 points a game. The Monarchs repeated its success with 34 wins, 1 loss, and its second national win.

"Her passion for athletics and enthusiasm for the game was contagious," said OD athletic director Jim Jarrett. "She was point guard and leader. She did so much more than score. She was a great passer and had the ability to get the ball inside to others to score. She played the game to win. That passion sold the game of women's basketball like it was never sold until that time."

Lady Magic

Old Dominion fans were used to Nancy's fancy passing. Then Magic Johnson and his Michigan State team came to play Old Dominion men. Reporters wrote how Magic passed like Nancy. They concluded that Nancy must be "Lady Magic." The nickname stuck.

Nancy's drive to compete and win created amazing interest in women's basketball. When she started at OD in 1977, about 350 people attended games. By the time she graduated four years later, games averaged 5,000 fans. The Lady Monarchs became one of the first women's college teams to have its games broadcast on television.

"She was an ambassador for the game," said OD's Debbie Bryner. "She made people want to watch and play. Her style as point guard was flashy, with behind-the-back passes and moves not usually done by women. She had appeal for the media. Her senior year, she handled 20 interviews a week, including television talk shows."

"She made people want to watch and play."

Nancy made All-American her last three years and OD Outstanding Female Athlete of the Year all four years. She received the 1979 Broderick Cup for top student athlete in the nation and was the only two-time winner (1978, 1979) of the Wade Trophy for outstanding female college basketball player. She remains OD's leader in career assists (961) and second in steals (512), and holds many single-game and single-season records.

"It was important to show people I could do anything I want if I believe in myself and make the commitment," Nancy stressed.

Turning Professional

Nancy left OD at a good time. The Women's Professional Basketball League had already been going for two years. Nancy joined the league's Dallas Diamonds in 1980, beginning her two-decade uphill battle to forge a professional basketball career. The first year with the Diamonds, she led the team in scoring, averaging 32 points a game. She also steered the team to a division title and was named Rookie of the Year. Nancy was hot, but the league died the next year.

Nancy stayed in Dallas, taking various sports-related jobs. She reported television sports and helped tennis star Martina Navratilova stay in shape. Meanwhile, Nancy played pickup basketball games whenever she could.

In 1984, Nancy joined the Dallas Diamonds once again. This time, the team was part of the new Women's American Basketball Association (WABA). Nancy took the rebuilt Diamonds to victory in the league championship over Chicago. That year, she outscored teammates for a second time, averaging 27 points a game. But the WABA went broke before another season.

Unlike other women basketball players, Nancy refused to go overseas. Her roots were in the United States. She believed that if she worked hard enough, something would happen for her here. She was right.

Playing with the Big Boys

In 1986, Nancy received an invitation to play with the Springfield Fame, a men's summer professional team. She became the first woman to play—and start—in a men's league. Although teammates accepted her, Nancy found the experience frustrating. The men were stronger and quicker. They could block her shots more easily. Still, Nancy knew that her addition to the team helped change the public's view of women playing basketball.

Nancy stayed with the Fame for two years. Then she joined the Washington Generals, a show team that traveled with the famous Harlem Globetrotters. The Generals' job was to entertain fans and make the clowning Globetrotters look good. Nancy worried that the slapstick play was making her skills sloppy. The constant touring proved tiring. But at least she had found a place to play basketball—for a year.

Time for Other Things

In 1988, Nancy married former Washington Generals teammate Tim Cline. Seven years later, they had their son, Timothy Joseph (TJ). During that time, Nancy found new ways to make a living with basketball. She continued her television broadcasting career, reaching fans through five different networks. Companies hired her to talk about sports and their basketball

In 1997, 38-year-old Lieberman-Cline became a guard with the Phoenix Mercury and WNBA's oldest player.

products. Nancy organized her own company to promote sports, wrote books and newspaper articles about how to play, and held clinics and camps for basketball lovers like herself.

All the while, she worked out five days a week to keep in shape—just in case. Still, she talked about retiring from playing for the first time. Maybe she would coach full time. As long as she could be around basketball, she would be happy.

In 1992, Nancy toured with Athletes in Action. This team of former college stars traveled around the country to scrimmage with the nation's top college teams. Nancy proved she still had the magic touch. She averaged 16 points, 6 rebounds, 6 assists, and 2 steals a game.

The Comeback Kid

By 1997, Nancy was pretty much retired. The past year she had been inducted into the Naismith Basketball Hall of Fame and the New York City Basketball Hall of Fame, the first woman to receive the honor. Then, the WNBA launched its new league. In her heart, Nancy still wanted to play. Once again, she heard: "You'll never be able to do this."

"People said, 'You don't want to embarrass yourself,'" Nancy admitted. "My husband asked, what if people remember, and you don't play at that level. I told TJ to tell his dad I was going to play. I love those challenges."

Nancy canceled speaking engagements to devote time to getting in shape. She hired a basketball trainer and strength coach. She spent months on the court with 6-foot to 6-foot, 9-inch junior college players near her Dallas home. She practiced her jump shots, behind-the-back and cutting passes, and steals.

Once again, hard work paid off. At age thirty-eight, Nancy became the oldest player in the WNBA, taking a spot as guard with Arizona's Phoenix

Mercury. At her opening WNBA game, fans found Nancy's skills better than ever. She played a solid 37 minutes and wound up with 14 points and 7 assists, not the numbers of a has-been. She finished the season with averages of 8 points, 3 rebounds, 3 steals, and 3 assists. Nancy proved that age means nothing compared to hard work.

The Coach

After the season ended, the thirty-nine-year-old received an offer from the WNBA to manage and coach a new team, the Detroit Shock. She could still continue her other basketball projects. But she would split her time between homes in Dallas and Detroit.

Nancy found the decision difficult to make. She had hoped to play one more season. "But I also knew ... I didn't want to be known as someone who was just hanging around," Nancy told a reporter. "This is another way to contribute to the sport." In the end, she accepted the job.

Nancy quickly discovered that coaching was a natural next step in her incredible career. She brought the same passion to coaching that she had given on the court, leading her team to the playoffs their second year as a team.

"There is nothing that excites more than being on the sideline coaching and sharing and teaching," Nancy decided.

Coach Lieberman-Cline encourages the Detroit Shock from the sidelines.

In 1999, Nancy joined the first group of women inducted into the Women's Basketball Hall of Fame. The hall highlighted her many groundbreaking achievements. The ten-year-old who vowed to make basketball history had fulfilled her promise by becoming a basketball legend. No other player had a national athletic award named after them. With every breakthrough, Nancy had attracted millions of fans to the women's game, opening doors for today's basketball stars. And she is not through yet.

"I am trying to build a championship team. I would like to be a great mom, and I would like to help women in sports. I want to help all sports grow and be a good role model for kids as well as for women. If people view me as someone who opened doors, I am happy. Every day I try to make a difference."

NANCY'S OTHER INTERESTS:

Playing basketball any time any place; being mom to son, Timothy Joseph (TJ).

NANCY'S BASKETBALL TIP:

Never stop working, wanting, or dreaming. You have to work to be good. You have to dream to set your goals. And you have to want to accomplish your goals.

Chapter Four

Sheryl Swoopes

Reporters call Sheryl Swoopes "the best woman basketball player." Many believe she is the reason why women's basketball is so popular today. Her shooting eye, her dazzling charges, her drive to compete and command the game—these are qualities that thrill fans and help teammates win championships. These are the strengths that broke high school, college, and WNBA records, setting Sheryl apart from other players.

"Sheryl is an all-around player," WNBA Houston Comet teammate Jennifer Rizzoti told a reporter. "She gets the job done on both ends of the floor and does whatever it takes for us to win."

Cheering for Basketball

Sheryl was born on March 25, 1971, in the small, dusty farm town of Brownfield, Texas. As a young girl, she never dreamed of becoming a basketball star. She pictured herself as a nurse or flight attendant or, best of all, a cheerleader. When two of her three older brothers shot baskets at school games, Sheryl danced around the gym—cheering.

When she got older, Sheryl often watched James and Earl practice after school. As they fired balls into a makeshift hoop in their rocky backyard, she wanted to play, too. But they refused to let their sister shoot. They said that basketball was for boys.

Sheryl begged and pleaded until they let her play. Still, they teased her with rough games of keep-away, expecting her to quit. But Sheryl began to really like basketball, so she stayed in their games no matter how many times they pushed and bumped her. Because the boys couldn't get rid of her, they taught her the rules of the game. They never let her win, but Sheryl learned to dribble and shoot the ball. Their games made her tough.

At seven years, Sheryl joined the Little Dribblers, a local girls' basketball team. Playing with girls seemed easy compared with her brothers' rough-and-tumble game. Within a year, Sheryl led the Little Dribblers to national championships in Beaumont, Texas. The team lost in the final game, which saddened Sheryl. This was her first of many ups and downs with basketball.

Meanwhile, Sheryl's dream of cheerleading faded. The closest she ever came to cheerleading was the pep squad in sixth grade. Her older cousin supplied the uniform. Otherwise, the family could never have afforded the clothes and pom-poms.

Sheryl's dad, Billy, had left home when she was a baby, so money was always tight. Her mother, Louise, raised Sheryl and her brothers alone in a three-room house. She worked two jobs to make ends meet. Some months the family needed public assistance just to eat. Sheryl went without new clothes, cars, vacations, and other extras her friends took for granted. Still, she drew strength from her mother's ability to keep their family together and thriving. From her, Sheryl learned the value of family, hard work, and the simple things in life.

High School Hoops

In junior high school, "Legs," as her friends called her, played basketball and volleyball. By ninth grade, Sheryl decided to focus on basketball. The summer before high school, she pushed to better her skills during playground pickup games with the boys. Like her brothers, these guys rarely gave her a chance to play. But the occasional extra workouts helped her improve.

Sheryl easily made the junior team at Brownfield High School. After only one game, the coach bumped her up to the top varsity team. She was quick; she sank baskets. After years of getting around taller, stronger boys, Sheryl proved unstoppable on the girls' team. By her second year at Brownfield, she was 6-feet tall and clearly the best player on the team.

"It helps to play with the guys," Sheryl explained to a reporter. "They are so much more physical than girls are. Once you play with guys and you get in a situation with girls, you think, 'Well, if I scored on that guy, I know I can score on her.'"

"It helps to play with the guys."

Away from the court, Sheryl ran track and studied. "Legs" recorded the farthest long jump in Brownfield history. She was also a good student. She had to be. Louise Swoopes set strict rules for her children, with early curfews and no sports unless homework was finished. Still, the bubbly athlete found time for many friends. One special friend, Eric Jackson, became her boyfriend.

The Brownfield Cubs went to state basketball championships three of Sheryl's four years. During her third year, the Cubs played Hardin-Jefferson, the top-ranking team, for the finals. By the end of the first half, the Cubs trailed Hardin by six points. Sheryl refused to give up. She stormed through the second half, firing balls until the Cubs took the lead and won. Sheryl wound up the only player to score more than 9 points, recording an amazing 26 points with 18 rebounds, a Brownfield record. The state of Texas named her high school player of the year.

Colleges Come Calling

News of the girl basketball wonder spread. At sixteen years, reporters compared her to one of basketball's finest, Michael Jordan. Her ability to play any position well and sense of competition reminded fans of Jordan. The publicity proved helpful for attracting interest from colleges nationwide. The only way Sheryl could afford to go to college was through athletic scholarship. Of all the colleges that came calling, Sheryl chose the University of Texas for its great courses and basketball team.

With college set, Sheryl turned her attention to winning another state championship. This time, something went wrong. The Cubs lost in the district finals. Sheryl blamed herself, much as she had with the Little Dribblers.

"I played poorly and once again had a sick feeling inside that I let everyone down," she wrote in her book *Bounce Back*. But only Sheryl felt she had failed. She graduated from Brownfield with averages of 26 points, 14 rebounds, 5 assists, and 5 steals per game—not the numbers of a loser.

College Changes

The University of Texas turned into another surprise. From the beginning, Sheryl felt out of place. The Austin, Texas campus was huge. Sheryl missed her family and Eric, still her boyfriend. After less than one week on campus, she flew home and never returned.

Sheryl enrolled in South Plains Junior College, just 30 miles from Brownfield in Levelland, Texas. Coach Lyndon Hardin was thrilled to have such a tremendous athlete on the Lady Texan basketball team.

"She was a lot of fun to coach because she was so talented," Hardin recalled. "Her quickness, the ease she accomplished things. We used her in the inside game. She was a good enough ball handler that she could play guard as well. She is probably the most versatile athlete in terms of playing every position on the floor that I have ever coached."

Sheryl shone at the two-year college. She was a solid student who easily won people over with her smile. With basketball, however, she was over the top.

In 52 games over two seasons, she averaged 26 points a game. She set 15 records, including the most career points (1,554); achieved junior college all-American in 1990 and 1991; and was named the 1991 junior college player of the year.

"She had a high-point game of 45 points but could have had 55," Hardin boasted. "She was an unselfish player. She gave up the ball five or six times so others could score. She never set out to break records; they just happened."

Big-Time College Basketball

After two years at junior college, Sheryl felt prepared to tackle a larger school and more cutthroat competition. In 1991, she transferred to Texas Tech University in Lubbock, Texas. Before Sheryl arrived, opponents thought of Texas Tech's Red Raiders as a minor regional problem. Two years later, the Red Raiders turned into a national powerhouse. The difference was Sheryl Swoopes, the 6-foot shooting guard and forward known as the Texas Tornado.

Sheryl was a regular point-scoring machine. She averaged 21.6 points a game during her first year. For the first time ever, Texas Tech reached the National Collegiate Athletic Association (NCAA) regional semifinals. Sheryl's second year proved even more incredible. The team won 12 games and lost only 3, sending Sheryl and her teammates to the regional conference.

To Sheryl's alarm, the final game pitted her against the University of Texas, the school she had left. She threw herself into the game, hoping to prove that she had made the right decision by leaving. Sheryl scored a career and NCAA game high of 53 points, and the Red Raiders won, sending them to their second NCAA playoff.

Four wins later, the Red Raiders faced Ohio State in the title game. Sheryl played her heart out, trying not to repeat the losses suffered in final games with the Little Dribblers and Cubs. After seeing her sink 10 baskets in a row, teammates kept sending her the ball to beat down Ohio. The plan worked. When the final buzzer blared, the score was 84–82. Texas Tech had earned its first national title, and Sheryl had sunk an NCAA championship record of 47 points.

"It was absolutely one of the great all-time performances in basketball," Nike's Sue Levin declared.

Killing Time

The 1992–93 basketball season brought Sheryl a host of honors. She ranked as the NCAA's second highest scorer—man or woman—averaging 28.1 points a game. She won almost every women's athletic and basketball award and player of the year tributes from nine organizations, including the Woman's Sports Foundation. Nike officers, who were struck with Sheryl's talent and character, offered to pay her to represent their clothes and shoes.

Once the excitement fizzled, however, Sheryl found nowhere to go with her talent. The only way she could earn a living shooting hoops was to follow basketball overseas. The fall of 1993, Sheryl left for Italy to play with the Basket Bari. She played ten games, averaging 23 points a game. Then contract problems sent her home.

Sheryl returned to Texas Tech to complete her college degree. To earn money, she worked at a Lubbock bank and broadcasted college radio games. She continued to speak on behalf of Nike, who expanded her contract to include an Air Swoopes shoe. Air Swoopes became the first basketball shoe named for a woman athlete.

Sheryl also taught at summer basketball camps. One camp was run by Michael Jordan. Jordan arranged for Sheryl to compete against him one-on-one in front of his campers and television cameras. During the game, Sheryl sank the first three baskets. Then they exchanged hoops until Jordan tried to break away with his high-jump dunks. On his first leap, Sheryl caught him around the waist and held him down.

"Oh my gosh, I just fouled Michael Jordan!"

"I surprised both of us," she wrote. "I thought, 'Oh my gosh, I just fouled Michael Jordan!'" The game ended with Michael winning, but only by 7–5.

Road to the Olympics

Throughout her time without a team, Sheryl focused on keeping in shape for the 1996 Olympic team tryouts. She had tried out for the U.S. Olympic team in 1992, but a last-minute injury kept her off the team. Now was her chance. Sheryl worked on speed and weight training to build up her 145-pound frame. All the while, she worried that her lack of international contests put her at a disadvantage against older, more experienced players. She had helped the U.S. national team win a bronze medal in Australia and the gold at the Goodwill Games. But most of her teammates played regularly on overseas teams.

To practice, Sheryl competed in nightly pickup games at the local recreation center with wanna-be athletes. The problem was that these games could get rough for a woman. Eric, her boyfriend, now doubled as her trainer and bodyguard.

"I'm out there for security reasons," he told *Sporting News*. "She'll go by some of the guys and embarrass them. Maybe the next time down, she's going in for a layup, and there's a hard foul. That's when I have to step in."

In June 1995, Sheryl married her longtime boyfriend. The same month, she attended 1996 Olympic basketball tryouts in Colorado. For one week, 27 women competed for 12 positions. Sheryl had never worked so hard. Her reward was a spot on the U.S. Olympic team.

Olympic Gold

Sheryl practiced with her teammates for three months. Then, the women spent nine months playing 52 pre-Olympic games against college and international teams. The coach sent Sheryl in for an average of 21 minutes a game. In that time, the flexible forward and guard averaged 12 points and 4 rebounds while leading the team in steals.

By the Atlanta Olympics, Sheryl was pumped. The U.S. women easily defeated seven teams leading into the finals. Sheryl averaged 12.6 points a game. Her job in the finals against Brazil was to guard their top shooter. But in the first few minutes of the game, Sheryl fouled twice and was benched. She feared that she had messed up the game of a lifetime. Then the coach sent her in again. This time, Sheryl scored 16 points, helping her team beat Brazil 111–87.

Sheryl accepted her gold medal with tears in her eyes. She thought of the sacrifices she and Eric had made for basketball. She remembered the long months of training and life on the road. Everything seemed small compared with the thrill of representing the United States for its first gold medal since 1988. That night, Sheryl slept with the medal under her pillow.

Basketball Mom

The Olympics highlighted Sheryl's bulldozing talent and upbeat personality. She would be a big draw for either the ABL or WNBA league. Each wanted her to

> *"There were a lot of people who had doubts that ... I would be able to come back."*

sign with them. After much thought, Sheryl chose the WNBA's Houston Comets. The team was Texas based, closer to home.

The Comets kicked off their first season in June 1997. But the popular Olympian delayed her part in the WNBA season. On June 25, 1997 Sheryl gave birth to son Jordan, who was named after buddy Michael Jordan. Six weeks later, Supermom joined the Comets on the court for a game with the Phoenix Mercury. Not only did the Comets win the game, but Sheryl helped the team claim its second league title.

"There were a lot of people who had doubts that after I missed almost an entire season, after having my child, that I would be able to come back. Not only to play, but to be in the shape I was in before, and to be able to be the old Sheryl Swoopes," she bubbled.

From then on, Sheryl juggled being a star athlete and mother. When she went on short trips, Jordan came along and a nanny took care of him. That way, Sheryl could think about her job but have him close. For longer trips, Jordan stayed at home with his father or grandmother.

Having a child deepened Sheryl's pledge to make children come first. She determined to be the role model for young girls that she never had.

Sheryl high-jumps for the ball, towering over Sting players in a 1998 game.

WNBA All-Stars

Sheryl often pushed herself beyond what her body could take. In one July 1998 game against Sacramento, she fainted from lack of fluids. Three days later she returned to the court, scoring 18 points in 22 minutes and recording her career high of 7 assists.

Off-season, Sheryl never seemed satisfied with her playing. To improve, she ran, rode a bike, and played pickup ball with guys five days a week. "I wanted to get stronger than last year when I was one of the worst rebounders in the league," she admitted. "I concentrated on defense. I felt if I could get my defense going, I could score some points. And I wanted to be able to shut down the other teams' best players."

To fans, Sheryl's game seemed fine just the way it was. In 1999, the WNBA called for votes to create its first all-star game. Out of more than one million votes cast in 12 WNBA cities, Sheryl received the highest number (84,632). "I was very, very shocked and very honored," Sheryl said in her usual modest way. "To me, it showed that no matter what I think, the general public sees the hard work I put into the game."

Hoop History

Once again, Sheryl's extra effort paid off. In June 1999, the Comets, who set a league record of 15 wins in a row in 1998, posted their second straight victory of the 1999 season. Sheryl scored 21 points with 6 assists, 5 rebounds, and 3 steals to help her team beat the Washington Mystics 88–63. Her lightning game seemed better than ever.

The evening had its bittersweet moments. Sheryl and her husband had announced their divorce. For the first time, Eric's support was gone.

"He was at every game. It's completely different this year. It's something that as the season goes on, and we play more games, I'll be able to handle," Sheryl told reporters.

Sheryl rebounded from her problems by making history once again. On July 11, 1999, she accomplished the first triple-double in the WNBA. That meant she recorded points, rebounds, and assists all in the double digits. The Comets clobbered the Detroit Shock 85–46, with Sheryl managing 14 points, a career-high 15 rebounds, and 10 assists.

Sheryl outruns Vicki Johnson in a 1999 game against New York Liberty.

The Future

Sheryl remains one of the most popular basketball players—woman or man. Her original Air Swoopes shoe comes in five different styles. Her name graces three basketballs, a jersey, children's books, trading cards, a phone card, and an action figure, and the list keeps growing.

Right now, Sheryl is at the top of her game. She helps teammates score; she shoots two for three from the free-throw line; and her rebounds drive the game.

"I know she's a complete player," Comets teammate Jennifer Rizzoti says. "From everybody I've talked with who was on the team last year and had seen her play in the past, they've said she's taken her game to another level."

There is no stopping the Texas Tornado.

SHERYL'S OTHER INTERESTS:

Son Jordan; volleyball, track, softball; shooting pool.

SHERYL'S BASKETBALL TIP:

Set high goals for yourself. Do something every day to improve.

Chapter Five

Lisa Leslie

Most people dream of becoming the best in one career. Lisa Leslie shoots for the stars in two—basketball and modeling. So far, the 6-foot, 5-inch center has made her dreams come true. Lisa elegantly poses for photographers and acts on television. At the same time, she sets records and outscores opponents, whether at the 1996 Olympics or with the WNBA's Los Angeles Sparks.

"Lisa is a great player and Olympian and a successful WNBA player," says former Olympian and University of Tennessee coach Pat Summit. "She's done modeling. She is great with kids and adults. She's a great role model for our sport."

Raised on Pride and Hard Work

Lisa was born on July 7, 1972, to Walter Leslie, a former semiprofessional hoopster, and Christine. The family, which included Lisa's five-year-old sister, Dionne, lived in Compton, California, a town near Los Angeles. When Lisa turned four, her father left home for good. Christine raised their daughters herself, determined to build a close-knit family.

At first, Christine Leslie took a job as a letter carrier. A babysitter watched the girls and made sure they completed their chores. At night, an exhausted mother helped her daughters with homework. She expected them to work hard and take pride in what they accomplished.

Christine also taught her daughters to be proud of their height. By the time she was in second grade, Lisa was the tallest person in her class. Kids teased her with names like beanpole or Olive Oyl, after the tall, skinny girl in *Popeye* cartoons. Christine knew about teasing, too. She was 6 feet, 3 inches, and Walter had been 6 feet, 5 inches. She told the girls that being tall showed that they came from African royalty, and they should celebrate their height. Each fall, she had them model their new school clothes in a pretend fashion show. Christine gave them lessons from a former model at a local charm school. Then, she pointed out how no matter what job she did, she was all woman, complete with styled hair and polished nails. Lisa listened to what her mother said. She wanted to be a model.

"The closer I got to my mother's height, the more beautiful I felt," Lisa told a reporter.

Moving Around

In 1982, Christine learned that her job might end. Rather than wait to be laid off, she sold the house and bought an 18-wheel truck. She hired a live-in babysitter to take care of Lisa, Dionne, and their two-year-old sister, Tiffany. Then she started a new career as a long-distance truck driver. The new job brought more money. But it meant that Christine traveled far from home for days at a time. Lisa missed her mother terribly when she was gone.

"There were some sad times," she explained to a reporter. "But we understood. It made me mature really fast."

During the summer, Lisa and her sisters packed into the truck and drove cross-country with their mother. At night, the five shared a bunk in the cab of the truck. The space was tight, but at least the family was together. Lisa saw much of the nation that way.

The summer trips worked until the girls became too big for one small bunk. Christine arranged for Lisa and her sisters to live with their aunt and her kids in Carson, a town near Los Angeles. The girls had moved often because of their mother's work. In one three-year period, Lisa changed homes three times and schools four.

Lisa always seemed to see the bright side of every move. The only thing that got her down was being asked the same question: "Do you play basketball?" By seventh grade, Lisa was 6-feet, 2-inches tall. Everyone assumed that someone so tall should play basketball. Lisa was so sick of being asked that she never wanted to play.

One day, Lisa decided to shoot hoops with a group of boys at the park—just to try the game and shut people up. She stood 6 inches taller than the boys, so she scored easily. The boys taught her to rebound and block shots. She discovered that basketball was fun after all. Lisa returned to the park often, eventually joining an all-boys' team.

The next year at Whaley Junior High School, Lisa tried out for the eighth-grade girls' basketball team. She was surprised how well the girls played. Lisa, on the other hand, relied on her height. Although she made the team, Lisa worked hard to learn the fine points of basketball. The fact that the team won every game helped keep her interested.

When the season ended, Lisa told her cousin, Craig Simpson, how much she missed playing. Craig played basketball in high school. He knew what a good player a girl over 6 feet could be. He offered to work with Lisa to improve. He gave her exercises to strengthen her body. He taught her different passes, jumps, and better ways to shoot. Then he taught her to be tough by having her practice with older boys.

"Working with my cousin is how I got my skills," Lisa admitted later.

One More Move

The summer of 1986, Lisa's family moved to Inglewood, another suburb of Los Angeles. Lisa started at Morningside High School the following fall. A week into classes, she tried out for and made the Lady Monarchs, one of the best basketball teams in southern California.

"As a player, she was tremendous from day one," Coach Frank Scott recalled. "She was rough and needed work. But she was a hard worker, and you could see her improve day by day."

Lisa was a standout player from her first game. Her job as center was to grab rebounds and block shots. Lisa's training with boys had prepared her to play a more forceful game. When she caught the ball near the basket, she almost always scored. By her second year, Lisa seemed unbeatable. She was fast, powerful, and, by now, 6 feet, 5 inches.

Lisa helped her team to the state championships. The Lady Monarchs played their final game with the team from Fremont. At halftime, Morningside led by 10 points. But in the last minute, Fremont pulled ahead by one point.

"I told everyone to give Lisa the ball," Coach Scott said. "She took the last shot and missed. We lost 54–53. That stuck with her a while. After that, she worked even harder because she wanted a repeat of that game. The next year we went back to state, and she dominated with 21 points and 14 rebounds. We beat Fremont 60–50."

All-Around Teenager

By her senior year, Lisa was considered the best basketball player in the area. College coaches called almost daily to entice her with scholarships to attend their schools. Lisa's mother pushed her daughter to keep her grades high and try other activities. Otherwise, colleges would take back their offers.

Lisa maintained a 3.5 average, including many honors classes. A popular student, she was voted class president for three years. She also played volleyball and ran track, excelling in sprints and high

"I think it's cool to be feminine on the court. You can't judge people by how they look."

jumps. Being a limber jumper with great height allowed Lisa to slam-dunk. She became the first high school girl and second female of any age to dunk in a game.

Throughout high school, Lisa wore makeup on the court. Some kids complained, saying she wasn't serious about the game. But Lisa just liked to look nice. "On the court, I got the job done," she told a reporter later. "My hair was neat, my nails were polished, and I wore lipstick when I played. I think it's cool to be feminine on the court. You can't judge people by how they look."

The Junior Olympics

After Morningside beat Fremont in 1989, Lisa received an invitation to try out for the national team that would play in the Olympic Festival. The team was made up of the nation's best high school players. Lisa turned out to be so good that she made the junior team of college students instead.

That July, Lisa traveled with the team to the Junior World Championships in Bilboa, Spain. Although the United States only won 3 of 7 games,

Lisa proved a great talent. She averaged 13.3 points, 7 rebounds, and 3 blocks per game. She topped all players in free-throw shots, field goals, and steals. And she was the youngest player in the competition! The experience made her add basketball to her list of possible careers.

Lisa remained a powerhouse throughout her last year at Morningside. She dominated games, averaging 27 points and 15 rebounds. In one game, she scored 101 points in only 16 minutes of play. She would have continued to break the game record of 105 points made by basketball star Cheryl Miller, but the other team refused to play the second half of the game.

During her last state championship, Lisa finished with game highs of 35 points, 12 rebounds, and 7 blocked shots. The other coach admitted that none of his players could guard her. The amazing part of this game was how well Lisa played while having a case of chicken pox.

On to College

Of all the college offers, Lisa decided on the University of Southern California in Los Angeles (USC). It was a good school with a top basketball team, and it was close to home. Lisa found college an unexpected challenge. Schoolwork produced hours of studying each day, much more than at Morningside. The coach of the Lady Trojans set a demanding schedule of practices and games. Lisa pushed to stay focused.

From the beginning, Lisa amazed USC with her basketball. In her first game, she recorded 30 points, 20 rebounds, and 4 steals. Fans loved to see her lean body jump for a dunk. The coach quickly moved her to starting center. The Lady Trojans finished the season by making the NCAA tournament but losing in the first round.

Lisa continued to shine. She ended her first season with an average 20 points and 10 rebounds per game. She was chosen for the All-Pacific-10 team, which happened each of her years at USC, and she received the Pacific-10 National Freshman of the Year honor. By the end of her fourth season with the Lady Trojans, Lisa had averaged an amazing 21.9 points a game, and tallied a groundbreaking 95 blocks, a USC record that still stands. In several of her games, she topped 30 points, including one game that reached 34 points. People constantly compared Lisa to the USC legend Cheryl Miller, who was a four-time All-American, 1984 national college player of the year, and the first athlete—male or female—to have her number retired by the university.

"A lot of coaches have said I have the potential to be the kind of player who can help women's basketball reach more people," Lisa claimed. "All I can do is try to be the kind of player my team needs, and if that's what women's basketball as a whole needs—great!"

"All I can do is try to be the kind of player my team needs."

Lisa finished college as the Pacific's all-time leading scorer (2,414), rebounder (1,214), and blocker (321). She received several player of the year awards and captured the Broderick Award for the best national female basketball player. Equally important, she had led her team to an 89–31 record, which included four NCAA tournament appearances and one Pacific-10 win.

International Basketball

Like many women athletes in 1994, Lisa found she had nowhere to play basketball after college. She wanted to compete for the 1996 Olympic team, but tryouts were almost a year away. Instead, she tried out and made the national World Championship team.

Once again, Lisa showed that she could handle international competition. Even though she was the team's second-youngest player, she outperformed most teammates. Her role was to support the more experienced players. Yet, she recorded an average 10 points per game and grabbed the team's second highest number of rebounds. Lisa proved an all-around player in speed, jumping ability, passing, and shooting. The U.S. team wound up with a bronze medal. Lisa and her teammates vowed that the Olympics would end differently.

After the tournament, Lisa realized two things. She needed a paying job, and she needed to play basketball regularly to make the Olympic team. When an Italian team made her an offer, the twenty-one-year-old pounced on the deal.

Lisa spent one season in Alcamo, Italy with the team Sicilgesso. In Italy, the league followed international rules, which differed from those in the United States. The Italian team gave Lisa chances to perfect her game within a strong league under worldwide rules. As center, she averaged 22.5 points per game and 11.7 rebounds. She learned to like Italy, and she became one of the team's top players. By the end of the season, however, Lisa knew her place was at home. She wanted to win the Olympic gold for her country.

Olympic Gold

The experience overseas changed Lisa. Up until Italy, her game had relied more on accurate jump shots and fancy footwork than force. But toughness ruled on the court overseas.

"They don't call fouls as much, so the play gets rough," she admitted. "I came back with a new attitude."

Still, even at 6 feet, 5 inches, Lisa weighed only 170 pounds, not enough to scare opponents. To prevent getting banged around, she lifted weights daily. She exercised to boost her energy level. Lisa was in tip-top shape for the USA Olympic Team tryouts. In 1995, she easily made the U.S. team, happy for the chance to represent her country.

"I'm really excited to work with Lisa," USA head coach Nell Fortner said. "She has the size, speed, and quickness to be a threat to the best in the world. She ... is so dangerous anywhere on the floor, offensively and defensively, that she's just a tremendous asset to any team."

Lisa lived up to her coach's expectations. After a year in Italy and working out, she showed everyone she was no longer a support person. Instead, Lisa dominated the games. She outscored everyone on the undefeated 1995–96 national team, boosted her three-point shots, and charged wherever needed on the court.

At the 1996 Atlanta Olympics, Lisa led her team to victory every game. She averaged the most points per game (19.5) and was second highest in rebounds (7.3). In the opening game of the medal round, Lisa overpowered the Japanese. One after another, her teammates fed her the ball. Each time, Lisa scored. By the end of the game, the U.S. team had won 108–93, and Lisa had set an Olympic record of 35 points.

Lisa really wanted to beat Brazil. She had tasted a win since losing to Brazil the year before in the world games. She got her chance when the U.S. team faced Brazil again for the final Olympic game. At first, Lisa started slowly, not scoring for the first eight minutes. Then the memory of the earlier loss fueled her fire to win. She darted across the court, made quick, high jumps, and, best of all, sank an amazing 12 of every 14 shots. By the end of the game, Lisa had scored 29 points and 6 rebounds, and the United

Lisa overpowered Japan's team at the 1996 Olympics with her high jumps and sharp shots.

States had clinched the gold medal 111 to 87. Reporters called her the "greatest center in women's basketball."

Runway Queen

After the Olympics, everyone knew about the high-jumping Lisa Leslie. Lisa used the attention to launch her other dream career—modeling. She had already appeared on the cover of the fashion magazine *Vogue*. Now she signed a contract with a modeling agency.

Lisa brought something different to the sports world. Here was this hard-driving, airborne player who commanded her game. Once the buzzer rang, however, she transformed into a dazzling woman. Lisa felt comfortable dunking basketballs or gliding down runways in evening gowns and 4-inch heels. Fans liked both sides of her. So did the many companies that used her winning smile and star power to sell products, everything from action figures to athletic shoes.

""We have a lot of tall women in the sport," Pat Summit agreed. "At 6 feet, 5 inches, I don't think anyone carries herself any better than Lisa."

Lisa discovered she liked everything about modeling. "It gives me a chance to let people know that

> *"I also like to show girls that you can be tough and feminine, too."*

there's much more to Lisa Leslie," she noted. "I also like to show girls that you can be tough and feminine, too. We have to stop feeling that we've got to choose one thing and cut off our other options. You can be whatever you want to be."

Finally, a Women's Professional League

As Lisa built her modeling career, women's basketball gained two new leagues. Both wanted Lisa. After much thought, she finally decided to go with the WNBA, which planned to form a Los Angeles team, the Sparks. Lisa could stay close to home. She would be one of the three key league spokespeople, along with Sheryl Swoopes and Rebecca Lobo.

For two years, Lisa dominated her team as center. She became one of the most visible and popular players in the league. In 1999, fans voted her to start as center for the first WNBA all-star game. Lisa recorded 13 points, 5 rebounds, 1 assist, and 1 steal for the winning West team. Her team beat the East 79–61. Teammates voted Lisa the most valuable player.

As soon as the 1999 WNBA season ended, Lisa was on the road again with the national team. Everyone said she was playing at the top of her game. She led in scoring for international competitions and games against select teams—all to prepare for the 2000 Olympic Games.

Bright Future

Lisa bought a home in Ingelwood, California. Here she is close to the Sparks, her family, and Hollywood, where she has acted on television shows, such as *Sister, Sister; Moesha;* and *Hangtime.* Lisa views herself as a multi-talented athlete. "It's not just about basketball, even though that's my main career and main focus," Lisa told a reporter.

Lisa sees herself as an important role model for young people. She is a board member of her church and spends considerable time with foster children. She talks with students in classrooms about keeping a positive attitude, and holds basketball clinics for girls and boys.

"She's just a tremendous person," Coach Scott praises. "She always comes back (to Morningside) two

Lisa rests after a game with Cuba.

or three times a year. She donates tons in terms of money and equipment. She is a hard worker who would do anything for anybody."

One thing Lisa always does is sign autographs, especially for boys. "Twenty years from now," she explained to *People Weekly*, "if one of them is the guy making the corporate decision, I want him to say, 'Why shouldn't I give a woman the opportunity to play pro sports?'"

Whatever Lisa does, she uses her varied skills to be successful. She will always be confident, gutsy, smart, and womanly. Like famous woman athletes before her, she will continue to use her fame to help the sport of basketball grow.

"I like that I can help to change people's perspectives about what women can and cannot do," Lisa said. "And when my playing days are over, I hope people will remember me as the most versatile center ever to play the game, man or woman."

LISA'S OTHER INTERESTS:
Listening to rap and gospel music; going to movies, reading, and playing board games with my family.

LISA'S BASKETBALL TIP:
Learn to like yourself for who you are, and accept others for who they are.

Chapter Six

Rebecca Lobo

Anyone who knows women's basketball today knows Rebecca Lobo. She soared to fame with her undefeated college team. Then she amassed a winning streak of 102 games with her college, national, and professional teams. From the beginning, Rebecca's friendly personality, top grades, and strong family values made her a media darling. Her popularity gave women's college and professional basketball the attention they needed to attract fans and expand. Along the way, Rebecca became the most recent ambassador of women's basketball.

Close Family Ties

Rebecca was born on October 6, 1973. She lived in Granby, Connecticut, with her parents, RuthAnn and Dennis, and older brother and sister, Jason and Rachel. When Rebecca was two years old, the Lobos moved across the state line to the small town of Southwick, Massachusetts. Here she grew up in a strict but loving home surrounded by nature.

With few people or activities within walking distance, the family became each other's favorite playmates. Rebecca played board games and other outdoor kid games with Jason and Rachel. Most of all, they played sports. When Rebecca was seven, she and Rachel asked for football uniforms for Christmas. RuthAnn and Dennis were both teachers who supported all their children's interests. The girls received the uniforms.

By the time she was in third grade, Rebecca played sports nonstop. She dreamed of wearing New England Patriots or New York Giants football uniforms. She even wrote a letter to the Boston Celtics manager. In it, she assured him she was "going to be the first girl to play for the Boston Celtics."

Early on, Rebecca found the greatest pleasure from basketball. As long as she could remember, she spent hours at a time shooting baskets in the family driveway. Sometimes, she played with her brother, sister, or parents. Other times, she played by herself, happy for the chance to be alone with her thoughts.

"It was more than a game to me. It was a chance to escape and to dream," Rebecca wrote in her book *The Home Team.*

Tomboy

In 1982, not everyone agreed that girls could play the team sports Rebecca enjoyed. Granby Elementary School offered few opportunities for active girls. So Rebecca often joined the boys at recess for soccer and football games. After a while, her teacher called her over to criticize her for playing with the boys. She seemed particularly bothered that Rebecca was the only girl eating lunch with them. She called Rebecca a tomboy and ordered her to dress and behave more like a girl. When RuthAnn heard how this woman had insulted her daughter, she fumed with rage.

"Good thing my mom's message sounded louder in my head than my teacher's," Rebecca told a reporter. "Otherwise, I might have believed there was something wrong with a girl playing basketball."

The following year, Rebecca signed up for girls' basketball at the recreation center. Not enough girls showed an interest, so the team was canceled. RuthAnn refused to give up. She boldly signed Rebecca up for a boys' team where she was the only girl. Rebecca was tall for her age, talented in sports, and accepted by the boys.

High School Days

Southwick-Tolland High School gave Rebecca the variety of sports she craved. She played field hockey, softball, and, best of all, basketball. By now, she was over 6 feet tall. She easily made the top varsity team her freshman year. Moreover, she scored 32 points in her first high school basketball game.

"Rebecca had great size for high school, and she could score inside or outside. But she just had a great attitude," Southwick coach Jim Vincent noted. "She was a team player ... always willing to help people and put others before herself. She got more out of an assist than a basket."

Still, Rebecca averaged 30 points and 20 rebounds per game her first year. She dominated games, attracting the attention of reporters and fans.

"She was years beyond her age."

Teammates never seemed bothered by Rebecca's fame. They realized she was different from the beginning.

"She was years beyond her age," Coach Vincent revealed. "Early on, she set goals for herself ... to be successful in high school and go to a Division I college and help them attain a championship. She had a vision of a women's basketball team. She envisioned a lot before these things happened. And it all came true."

Throughout high school, Rebecca was an honor student. She played saxophone in the school band and continued with three sports. During her senior year, she traded softball for track, wanting to get in better shape for college. Even as a newcomer to track, she won the Western Massachusetts competition.

But basketball is where Rebecca really sparkled. By now, she stood 6 feet, 4 inches tall. She co-captained a team that was on the brink of a tournament run. She had scored a personal and school game high of 63 points and was close to breaking another scoring record.

"I didn't want her to go into the tournament with that kind of pressure," Coach Vincent recalled. "We were playing an away game, and she already had 50 points. She was only a few points away from a state record. We could have waited until a home game with lots of fanfare. But she just wanted to get it out of the way. That's the kind of person she was—without fanfare."

Rebecca ended her high school career with a total of 2,710 points. That was the most points earned by any boy or girl in the state of Massachusetts. Her state plus school individual and game records still stand today.

University of Connecticut

Rebecca received more than one hundred offers for college scholarships. She chose the University of Connecticut (UConn) in Storrs. The team was nationally known, and the school was only an hour's drive from Southwick. The short drive meant that her parents could attend basketball games.

Rebecca had hoped for a strong showing during her first game. Instead, she scored 10 points and fouled out after 26 minutes. "I didn't have a clue what college basketball was about," the french-braided forward wrote. "I knew it couldn't get any worse."

Rebecca was always hardest on herself. That first game pushed her to work harder. She wound up the season averaging 14.3 points with 7.9 rebounds a game, solid numbers for a freshman. In addition, she earned rookie of the year from the Big East Conference.

During the next 1992–93 season, Rebecca turned into a standout player. Many of UConn's best players had graduated. The coach used Rebecca to plow down the court so other teammates could score. He pushed her to be tougher mentally and physically.

He refused to rest her for very long. Other coaches noticed how Rebecca dominated the game and assigned two or three players to guard her.

"This meant there was more pressure on me to do well," Rebecca wrote. "Generally, this sort of responsibility and pressure doesn't come until you're a junior or senior."

Terrible News

With renewed confidence, Rebecca ended the season averaging 16.7 points and 11.2 rebounds a game. More important, she blocked 96 shots, a school record. The next season went even better. The Huskies posted one win after another.

On December 13, 1994, the Huskies defeated the Virginia Cavaliers in one of their roughest games that season. Rebecca overpowered the game with the most points, rebounds, and blocked shots. After the game, she patiently signed autographs, as always. When she greeted her parents, she expected they would celebrate together.

But RuthAnn needed to tell her daughter something. She had cancer that required surgery. Rebecca's eyes filled as RuthAnn kept talking. "The best thing you can do for me is to continue to work hard. You do what you have to do, and I'll do what I have to do."

RuthAnn's courage gave Rebecca a new fighting spirit. She studied and practiced more than ever. The next game with Boston was scheduled on the day her mother was to have a lump removed from her breast. To Rebecca's surprise, her mother appeared in the stands before the game. Her parents had never missed a game and wouldn't start now. RuthAnn made every game through three months of her treatment for cancer. For both women, basketball became a way to escape the terror of RuthAnn's terrible disease, at least for a while.

The Big Game

Rebecca led her team to a record 27-win and 2-loss season. The Huskies lost in the NCAA tournament before making the Final Four playoffs. Rebecca's numbers skyrocketed with career highs in field goals and free throws. "We can't let this feeling go away," she told a reporter.

> *"We can't let this feeling go away."*

The next season, the Huskies kept winning. Every competition brought another wave of media attention. At least four local television crews and countless newspaper and magazine reporters appeared at each game. When Rebecca started at UConn, games barely attracted 2,000 fans. Now almost 9,000 fans crammed into the stadium for home games.

The UConn winning streak had a tremendous impact on women's basketball. Rebecca, especially, stood for the best in women's sports. She was an honor student who happened to play a good game.

Rebecca and her teammates filled stadiums wherever they played. Young girls bought Rebecca Lobo posters for their rooms and wore her number 50 jersey. Everywhere Rebecca went, autograph seekers swarmed around her. For the first time in a long time, women's college basketball created a stir on a national level.

Rebecca led the Huskies through an undefeated season of 29 games. Yet Rebecca and the Huskies never got too sure of themselves. They still had to defeat their rival for the title, the powerhouse University of Tennessee. The first half of the national championship game went poorly. Eight minutes into the game, the famous center-forward received three fouls and was benched. By halftime, Tennessee led 38–32.

Rebecca returned to the game in the second half. In one four-minute stretch, she sank a crafty reverse lay-up, whirled around for a basket, and hit two 17-foot jump shots from the baseline. Then, with 28.9 seconds left in the game, she went to the free-throw line. UConn led by only three points. Rebecca steadied herself, knowing this was the most important moment in her college career. First, she sank one basket. Then another dropped through the net. The stadium erupted in wild cheers as UConn won 70–64, ending with a 35-game winning streak.

"A picture-perfect way for someone to end a career," Rebecca told waiting reporters. "We're undefeated. We're national champions."

An announcer broadcast through the din that Rebecca had just been named top player in the

Final Four. She ended the season as all-time UConn leader in rebounds and blocks and second best in points and games played. She received the Wade Trophy for outstanding basketball player, Naismith National Player of the Year, and many other top honors, including 1995 NCAA Player of the Year. She also achieved a degree in political science and a second Academic All-American honor for honor roll grades. For the first time, a two-time All-American athlete was also a two-time academic All-American.

After Graduation

The championship win brought a host of honors and invitations for speaking engagements. One hundred thousand people filled the streets of Hartford, Connecticut, the state capital, for the team's victory parade. Rebecca was featured in many magazines and on the David Letterman show. Reebok contacted her about a shoe contract. Rebecca even jogged with President Clinton.

The best news for Rebecca was hearing that her mother's cancer was gone. Publishers thought readers would like to know more about the story of both their winning journeys. Several approached the women to write a book together. They signed with the only publisher that would allow them to tell their own story without a professional ghostwriter. Rebecca's ability to earn a book contract for *The Home Team* at age twenty-one proved her popularity.

But Rebecca still faced the problem of what to do after college. She thought about playing overseas or becoming a broadcaster. Luckily, USA Basketball helped her decide. In May 1995, Rebecca received an offer to try out for the national team that would play in the 1996 Olympics.

Rebecca made the team. Yet she played only a minor role. At age twenty-two, she was the youngest rookie in a sea of talented women athletes. Most had acquired vast amounts of professional experience on overseas teams. They played a rougher, more physical game than at UConn.

Rebecca understood that, if anyone, she belonged on the bench. She was thrilled just to be part of such an inspiring group of women athletes. But life was difficult going from number 1 to number 12. At times, Rebecca scrambled to keep up with the team. Rumors spread that she only made the team because of her popularity.

Few fans or media realized how poorly she played. Even though she only played backup, Rebecca still became the center of media attention. Many worried that her star power would overwhelm the other players. But the players never seemed worried.

"We're thankful for it," former Stanford star Jennifer Assi told a reporter. "Rebecca's a good ambassador for the sport. The attention she gets has been helping our team a lot."

On to the Olympics

The U.S. team played 52 practice games, winning every one. The unbeatable team forced the nation to take women's basketball seriously. Suddenly, there was enough interest to attract backers as well. Soon two U.S. women's professional leagues appeared. Both offered Rebecca deals worth hundreds of thousands of dollars. Rebecca put her thoughts of playing overseas or sports broadcasting on hold. At least for a while, she could earn a living through basketball in the United States.

Rebecca took her time deciding which league to join. For now, she concentrated on the Olympics. To help her focus on the Olympic win, Rebecca slipped a photo of a gold medal into her gym bag. The good luck charm worked. The U.S. team won all their leadup games and the competitions in the 1996 Atlanta Olympics. Winning the gold capped a two-year run of 91 winning games for Rebecca. Meanwhile, her personal grace and improved skills earned her the respect of her teammates.

After the Olympics, Rebecca signed a contract to play with the WNBA's New York Liberty. The WNBA pinned the league's future on its three superstars: Lisa Leslie, Sheryl Swoopes, and the new but extremely popular Rebecca Lobo. Each captured a different image of women. Lisa radiated glamour and beauty. Sheryl stood for small-town hominess. Meanwhile, Rebecca beamed all-American girl next door, the one who excelled in whatever she touched.

Rebecca pulls ahead to score against the Sparks in a 1997 game.

The league used her broad smile in commercials and magazines to help gain publicity. Reebok named a shoe for her. And Rebecca launched a career in sports reporting for ESPN. Rebecca and her two WNBA mates ushered in a new brand of role model—one who wore her height, weight, and athletic frame proudly.

"People in the past said that if you're a female athlete, you can't be attractive or feminine," Rebecca told a reporter. "We're saying don't be afraid to be both."

WNBA

Again there was talk. Many feared that teammates would resent Rebecca being the center of attention. She never paid her dues sharpening her skills overseas as they had.

Rebecca proved her critics wrong from the beginning. During the 1997 season, she guided the Liberty to 11 straight wins. This run peaked a personal winning streak of 102 games. Along the way, Rebecca grabbed WNBA season highs of 8 rebounds and led the Liberty with 1.82 blocked shots.

The next season, Rebecca gained even more fans. She led the Liberty in field goal percentages (0.48), rebounds (6.9), and blocked shots (1.1). She wrote about basketball and her views of life on her Internet journal *the world according to me*. Off-season, she continued to report for ESPN and

Rebecca proved how tough she could be in a 1998 game against the Cleveland Rockers.

now Connecticut Public Television. Besides sports, she donated time and money to breast cancer support groups.

Time-out

On June 10, 1999, Rebecca injured her knee 20 minutes into Liberty's first game of the season. After the swelling reduced, she needed surgery. From then on, Rebecca hobbled to home games on crutches and sat on the sidelines. She still went to practices. But most of her time was spent on exercises to strengthen her knee. Throughout the ordeal, Rebecca continued to write her journal with the same cleverness and humor. Only now she called it her *world on one knee.*

A season off did little to lessen Rebecca's popularity. She remained one of the WNBA's most popular box office draws. Even on the injured list, she received a huge number of votes for the first east WNBA all-star team.

Rebecca kept her star power with companies, too. She had already shot an episode of the television show *Sister, Sister*, with teammates Lisa Leslie and Nikki McCray. The Mattel toy company hired her to promote its new WNBA basketball Barbie, and she appeared in car advertisements. Meanwhile, the twenty-five-year-old center stayed with the game by reporting NCAA games and working out her sore knee for hours each day. When not training, she brushed out her french braid and donned a business suit to speak before groups about the game she loved.

"If you go to Des Moines (Iowa) and poll 100 people on what player they've heard of, they mention Rebecca first or second," WNBA president Val Ackerman told a reporter.

Basketball player, author, broadcaster, company representative—Rebecca Lobo goes after it all. She looks forward to a strong showing in 2000 with the Liberty. As she wrote on her web site: "2000 is gonna be the year."

REBECCA'S OTHER INTERESTS:

Movies, plays, reading, writing in my Web journal.

REBECCA'S BASKETBALL TIP:

Become the best person you can be, someone who respects others as you respect yourself.

Basketball Talk

Glossary

backcourt the half of a court where a team is defending

center player nearest the basket who captures rebounds and shoots baskets from close range

double dribble occurs when a player dribbles the ball, catches it, and dribbles again, which breaks the rules

dribbling pushing or tapping the ball to the floor one or more times while moving along the court

forward player between the free-throw line and sideline who assists with shooting and catching the ball

foul occurs when a player pushes, holds, or hits someone on the other team

free throw an unchallenged shot taken from behind the free-throw line or foul line that comes after the referee calls a foul on the opponent

frontcourt the half of a court where a team is attacking

guard player who does much of the ball handling and covers the area between the half-court and free-throw lines

jump shot shooting technique that requires the release of the ball in the air after the player jumps upward on both feet

layup shooting technique that requires a step and pushing off with the ball

pivoting stepping with one foot while keeping the other on the ground

point guard player who handles the ball

rebound a missed shot that bounces off the rim or backboard and is caught by another player

shooting guard player who mainly shoots and passes

traveling walking or running while holding the ball, which is against the rules

triple-threat a position facing the basket that allows the player the option of shooting, passing, or dribbling

Basketball Connections

Where to Find More Information

Basketball Groups for Girls and Women

Women's National Basketball Association (WNBA)
Olympic Tower Building
645 Fifth Avenue
New York, New York 10022
(212) 688-9622
http://wnba.com

Launched in 1997 under the guidance of the National Basketball Association, this women's professional league seems to be thriving with 16 teams in key cities.

USA Basketball
One Olympic Plaza
Colorado Springs, Colorado 80909
(719) 632-5551
http://www.olympic-usa.org/sports

This group is the U.S. national governing body for basketball. It sets rules and organizes teams and championships for players at all levels, feeding the most talented athletes into the national Olympic team.

Women's Basketball Hall of Fame
700 Hall of Fame Drive
Knoxville, Tennessee 37915
(423) 633-9000
http://www.knoxvilletennessee.com

Opened in 1999, this independent organization honors women in basketball through interactive displays about the history of women in the sport, a Hall of Honor that features outstanding players, and exhibits that encourage future athletes. Besides visiting, anyone is welcome to send information about women to induct into the hall.

Basketball Canada
557 Dixon Road, Suite 102
Etobicoke, Ontario, Canada M9W 1H7
(416) 614-8037
www.basketball.ca

This is the Canadian governing agency for basketball. It creates programs for players of all levels and feeds outstanding athletes into Team Canada, the national and Olympic team.

Youth Basketball of America
10325 Orangewood Boulevard
Orlando, Florida 32821
(407) 363-9262
www.yboa.org

Established in 1989, this U.S. organization with branches worldwide offers league development, tournaments, educational clinics, and cultural exchange programs for kids who like basketball.

General Sports Groups for Girls and Women

Amateur Athletic Union (AAU)
of the United States
Walt Disney World Resort
P.O. Box 10000
Lake Buena Vista, Florida 32830-1000
(407) 934-7200

Since 1967, this group has been running youth, women's, and men's sports programs through 58 districts around the country. The AAU works with the Olympic committee to prepare athletes for Olympic games.

Canadian Association for the Advancement
of Women and Sport and Physical Activity
1600 James Naismith Drive
Gloucester, Ontario, Canada K1B 5N4
(613) 748-5793
caaws@caaws.ca

This organization is similar to the U.S. Women's Sports Foundation. It gives awards, inducts women into the Canadian Basketball Hall of Fame in Almonte, Ottawa, and works to make sure that girls and women receive a fair shake in sports.

National Collegiate Athletic Association (NCAA)
P.O. Box 6222
Indianapolis, Indiana 46206-6222
(317) 917-6222

This is the main organization that sponsors college sports.

Staying Hot
Further Reading

Bennet, Frank. *The Illustrated Rules of Basketball.* Nashville, TN: Ideals, 1994.

Christopher, Matt. *On the Court with Lisa Leslie.* Boston: Little, Brown & Company, 1998.

Holohan, Maureen. *Friday Nights by Molly* (fiction). Wilmette, IL: The Broadway Players, 1998.

Lobo, RuthAnn, and Lobo, Rebecca. *The Home Team.* New York: Kodansha, 1996.

Macy, Sue. *Winning Ways: A Photohistory of American Women in Sports.* New York: Henry Holt, 1996.

Miller, Faye Young, and Coffey, Wayne. *Winning Basketball for Girls.* New York: Facts on File, 1992.

Mullin, Chris. *The Young Basketball Player.* New York: Dorling Kindersley, 1995.

Ponti, James. *WNBA Stars of Women's Basketball.* New York: Pocket Books, 1999.

Stewart, Mark. *Lisa Leslie: Queen of the Court.* New York: Children's Press, 1998.

Swoopes, Sheryl, with Brown, Greg. *Bounce Back.* Dallas, TX: Taylor Publishing, 1996.

Bibliography

Books

Anderson, Dave. *The Story of Basketball.* New York: William Morrow, 1997.

Blais, Madeleine. *In These Girls, Hope Is A Muscle.* New York: Atlantic Monthly, 1995.

Goldstein, Sidney. *The Basketball Player's Bible.* Philadelphia: Golden Aura Publishing, 1994.

Jares, Joe. *Basketball: The American Game.* Chicago: Follett Publishing, 1971.

Kessler, Lauren. *Full Court Press.* New York: Dutton, 1997.

Layden, Joe. *Women in Sports.* Santa Monica, CA: General Publishing, 1997.

Lieberman, Nancy. *Basketball My Way.* New York: Charles Scribner's Sons, 1982.

Smith, Lissa. *Nike Is a Goddess: The History of Women in Sports.* New York: Atlantic Press, 1998.

Woolum, Janet. *Outstanding Women Athletes.* Phoenix: Oryx Press, 1998.

Periodicals

Coffey, Wayne. "Lobo takes a long, hard road trip to Olympics." *Knight-Ridder/Tribune News Service,* 18 July 1996.

Davies, Erin. "Heir Jordan." *Texas Monthly,* June 1999, vol. 27, issue 6, p. S30.

Duffy, Mary. "Center of attention: Rebecca Lobo has become the poster girl for women's basketball and the sport couldn't ask for a better role model." *Women's Sports & Fitness,* March 1996, vol. 18, no. 2, p. 68(4).

Fornek, Scott. "Girls Got Game." *Chicago Sun-Times,* 18 July 1999.

Huntington, Anna Seaton. "So I wanna be a superstar; you got a problem with that?" *Women's Sports & Fitness,* November-December 1996, vol. 18, no. 8, p. 50(2).

Knisley, Michael. "'Swoopes' Dreams." *The Sporting News,* 22 May 1995, vol. 219, no. 21, p. 53(2).

Lambert, Pam. "Woman Warrior." *People Weekly,* 30 June 1997, vol. 47, no. 25, p. 109(2).

Lidz, Franz. "Mixing It up with the Guys." *Sports Illustrated,* 23 June 1986, vol. 64, p. 64(2).

"Lisa Leslie." *Current Biography Yearbook,* 1998, p. 375(3).

"Rebecca Lobo." *Current Biography Yearbook,* 1997, p. 330(4).

"Sheryl Swoopes." *Current Biography Yearbook,* 1996, p. 559(3).

"Talk to the Stars." *Sports Illustrated for Kids,* November 1996.

Truex, Alan. "Swoopes Proves Size No Advantage for Foe." *Houston Chronicle*, 18 June 1999.

Williams, Lena. "Teamwork off the Court." *The New York Times*, 21 August 1999.

Web Sites

Sports A to Z
http://www.olympic-usa.org/sports/az-3_4_1.html

Just Sports For Women
http://www.justwomen.com/justhoops.html

USA Basketball
http://www.usabasketball.com/usa_bios

WNBA Player Directory
http://www.wnba.com/playerfile/profile

Huddlin with the Pros
http://www.huddlin.com/v2/lisa.htm

ESPNET SportZone Team USA Biographies: Basketball
http://espn.go.com/editors/atlanta96/bios/wbask/leslies.html

Index